ND
The White Line of Language

Deb Stewart

The White Line of Language

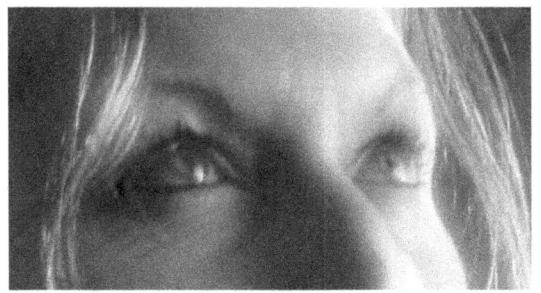

Acknowledgements

Some of the poems in this collection have appeared in *Slow Notes* (2008), *Shadow Selves* (2003), Friendly Street Poets anthologies, *Mascara Literary Review*, *Cordite*, *The Adelaide Review* (1989), *Transnational Literature*, *Indigo Book of Australian Prose Poems* (2011) *Memory video poetry* (2010), *Creatrix*, *On Tap* (1995), *Sleeping Under a Grand Piano* (1999), CCMixter.org and other print and online publications.

For Ash

The White Line of Language
ISBN 978 1 76041 746 8
Copyright © text Deb Stewart 2019
Cover and internal photos: Deb Stewart
Back cover photo of the author courtesy of Lucinda Corin

First published 2019 by
GINNINDERRA PRESS
PO Box 3461 Port Adelaide 5015
www.ginninderrapress.com.au

Contents

Automatic (Life) Writing	9
Drifting Toward Light	11
Slow Notes	18
Love	19
Hail	20
After the Weekend	21
Red	22
Penelope Sailing	23
To the Shadow of Myself	25
Oedipus and Electra	26
Red Booth	27
Lonely Women	28
Mid Drift	29
Argument	30
Holiday	31
Stranger	32
Slipping Out	33
When I was your mother	35
Ashes	36
Ghosts	37
Shuttlecock	38
I Killed a Bee	39
Home From the Hunt	41
Night Shoot	43
The Gun	44
Syrinx	45
Zen and the Art of Cleaning	49
Lava and Rain	50
The Street at Five a.m.	51
The River	52
Hawkesbury River Visit	53

River bend	56
Room	57
The Shy Girl	59
Dear Professor	61
Want	63
I want to kiss you	65
Rock	66
When you hold me	67
Sunday Morning	68
Google Earth	69
Inter Section (A Dream)	70
Dream	72
Scars	74
Only Thirty	75
The Search	76
The Weir	78
Relief	80
Miss Wiley Visits Springwood (1918)	83
This is where it begins	85
Something Like Egypt	88
The Pug Hole	89
All Roads Lead to Bombala	91
To Lake Pedder	93
Violet Town	94
Passing through the Suez Canal	96
Crossing the Equator	97
A Tourist in Te Aroha	99
Fish	100
Night Meditation	101
Big Sky	102
Guitar	104
Orange	105
Baptism	106

My Mother's Voice	109
There's a Strange Bird	110
Sheoak Guide	111
Surreal	113
Beach	114
Animal…Universe	115
Backwards	116
A Voice in the Night	118
The W(h)ishing of Rain	120
Outside Language	121
Water in a Blue Bowl	122
Winter Garden Meditation	123
Butterfly and bird – two haiku	124
A Poet's Self-defence	126
Dandelion Tea	127
Statice	128
The Swing	129
Love Poetry	130
Letter to an English Aunt	132
Book of Songs	134
One way to read poems	137
I am music	138
Ocean Woman	140
The Conversation of Cooks	142
Don't read poetry to me	143
Shared Music	144
Returning	145
Night Walk	147
Road Poem	148
White Mecca 1975	150
The End	152

Automatic (Life) Writing

…begin anywhere, accept whatever comes
what clichés, what golden images and
mixed metaphors the mind strums

begin anywhere　　　　　in spots of time
the cosmic catalogue of moments　epiphanies
snapshots cornered in albums
fading relatives curling like autumn leaves

seasons
years, lifetimes, amounting to
questions, accomplishments
childhood embarrassments –
fingers slip and tear
through wet painted butcher's paper
taped to preschool walls

awkward adolescence, yet moments of Glock sleekness
dangerous as a pistol with safety catch off
tight jeans and cigarettes, garage bands
musing on the ocean
contemplation　　　meditation
nights in phone boxes, moths beating at the glass
shiny black cord twirled on the wrist

writing poems through insomnia
can't beat Kerouac

his 94th chorus – 'Mexico City Blues'

'can't get on with my story,
write it in verse.
Worse.
Ain't go(t) no story, just verse'*

the broken narrative…plotless
guitar on the back steps under the moon
scribbling notes on a score
didn't understand half

old, new, borrowed and blue
white dress and carnations
ministrations
'Too young to be…'

so much unsaid
the purest, darkest thoughts unspoken
clipped language, the social glue of etiquette
political correctness   guarded spaces
hurtling toward death.

*From Jack Kerouac, 'Mexico City Blues' (94th chorus)

Drifting Toward Light

Nimbostratus

Not Churchill's *Black Dog*, but a bruise of a cloud
compresses all hope as it drifts above us again
and hovers indefinitely, the weather we must bear.
There's no snapping out of it as acquaintances suggest,
it will not be shaken or forcibly dispersed, but hangs
us in a limbo of stagnancy, where nothing new can grow.

It is the state of the weather, forecasted these past few years
since injury and chronic pain withdrew you from the world
throwing shadows over our dreams of a brilliant future.
Precipitation comes and goes, but barely reaches earth, and so
the soil of our existence thirsts for a cloudburst.

We can never know when it might pass forever, we dare not hope
for a few clear days seem to promise light, but then again
you wake with the dread of palpitations, stomach free-falling
and we know that Nimbostratus has descended.

Peace

Deep peace is all I wish for you.
You say it is all you want, but cannot attain.
The weather is out of control, your barometer will let you know
if rain is on the horizon, but cannot predict the Nimbostratus
    Blues.
I seem to harbour your pain in my own soul – can we be so close?
I translate it poetically, attempting to contain it in stanzas
and infuse it with a rhythm livelier than your own.
It flows through my fingertips and plays itself out on the fretboard,
its key is B flat and there's no joy in the composition.

Bouquet

It is my birthday, but you are immersed in the thickness of cloud.
So I go about my business – morning meditation, preparation
    for work.
The day is overcast, air heavy with the immanence of storm
I leave you in bed, the quilt a comfort moulded to your fetal form.
Later, arriving home, I smell the red wine staining your papers
but then the higher floral note of my birthday bouquet –
the shock a bright moment of colour shifting us closer to light.

If Only

Of all the if onlys there is one that matters –
if only the Nimbostratus Blues would dissipate
and leave us the clear blue score of the sky
on which to compose a future.

A Trio of Deaths

The light dazzled us for a while. You were almost yourself again
not quite the jester, but a purveyor of subtle sarcastic humour
the slightest hint of an upward curve teasing the corners of your mouth.
Then came a trio of deaths in little more than a week – two friends and a brother –
and a lifetime of grief. Difficult to speak, drawn back to memory,
a past of deep emotional connections like a child's eyelashes brushing a parent's cheek
the slightest but most profound stroke triggering a spiral of regret.
How quickly and completely we are submerged by sorrow. I feared you would never wake.

Flowers in the Night Sky

It is New Year's Eve and we attend our own quiet party of two
watching a rock concert on TV. The music is from a past
   generation,
the musicians of our youth returning decades older to
   perform enduring hits.
How do we endure the twisted path of time? Remembering,
   we are happy
and stories begin to unwind from us with the revolutions of
   our fan.

The night is hot and we know we will not sleep easily, yet we
   will try.
But first there is a New Year to see in and we walk across to
   the nearby oval
where there is an annual display of fireworks and music drifts
over darkened suburbs. It does not feel like a new beginning.
   We are afraid to dream,
and yet we are moved outside ourselves by the allure of
   flowers in the night sky.

Bliss

New Year's Day 2006

For rain
and relaxation
I am grateful

after heat
and fireworks,
New Year's Eve
indulgences

it is blissful
to lay about
and read,
to drift
into light sleeps

wake to raindrops
on acacia leaves
and shining agapanthus

sparrows playful,
joyous on tin roof
and in bird bath

the day is quiet
I listen to some poetry
I've taped
strum my guitar
wash lunch dishes
as though they were sacred objects

content with simplicity,
aware of deep peace
words flow
to become this poem
    bliss.

Slow Notes

You tell me
I cannot love you yet
with my one clipped wing
but you kneel –
cup the fallen bird
with reverence
and my slow notes
unfold
and sing.

Love

Didn't you say that love would enfold
not like a shroud but a holy wing –
that it was not too proud to declare itself
among jasmine and bees on the garden swing.

Why did it speak in a menacing voice
and press to the ear in an angry threat
veiled in whiskey and rolled cigarettes.

Why did it shatter my windows
and make me fear the force of your fist
raised through all my dreams.

Why did love breathe in laboured breaths
like a dying man in a narrow bed
just so much bone
in its rags of death.

Why did it hide in a shadowed place
as though it feared the light
and consume my body like a grave
as earth rained down on my face.

Hail

Cool night. He turns on the heater.
There's rain in the porch light.
The sky threatens hail.
She is there, in her jeans,
auburn hair in loose wet coils.
a month since they spoke.

His black windcheater, his three-day growth
reek of whiskey.
They circle each other
with half formed words.
Her voice soothing; his slurred.
Her breasts, through her sweater,
the musk of petals fallen in rain,
loosen his lips to a tender pout.

She wants to connect
but gets lost in his labyrinth of drunken logic
until, finally, all she can do is kneel at his feet
as he sits on the edge of the bed
and sobs into her hair.

A block away, a siren wails
for all the accidents of life.
She leaves the artificial warmth,
shuts the door on a world shattered by hail.

After the Weekend

We wind up, and over.

Paddocks sweep past, barren on our left.
To our right, the pine forest's dark.

I think it is finished.
In the dragging silence
I feel you anxious for other roads.

We replay separate memories
of the final argument.
Word for word,
your hand turning the wheel –
wordless.

Red

The day her boyfriend came home from gaol
she spilled out onto the quiet street
in a sheer red dress which showed
her flattened breasts, her bones
and the mad edge of her laughter
held itself to the neighbour's throats.

They all wished she would go back inside
and lie on her bed with a bottle of gin,
or sit in a haze on the lounge room floor
flicking her lighter at a pack of burning cards.

The street could not contain
the riot of her voice;
her stumbling red shape;
her bare white feet on their bitumen road.

They preferred the hysteric of her screams
bouncing off inner walls
of crushed and shattered plasterboard.
There a fist or two,
there the crater of a skull.
A whole panel gone
where he pushed her body through.

Her ecstasy lasted a day or two.
Then, in the middle of a night,
they screeched in the yard
like a pair of ill-matched cats
tearing at cloth; at hair and skin,
drawing each other's animal blood.

Penelope Sailing

… And I *am* Penelope
pushing out from your shore
no longer content

to weave a version of your life.
I have lived too long in your absence
clinging to myths of perfection
and fabulous homecomings.

The bed, your ally, is ever cold
freezing my affections
against hopeful suitors
who try to scale the palace walls.

There are moments
I *would* be held
and kissed by one
no more a stranger than yourself

But you are there
conquering oceans in my mind
discovering islands
drowning out the luring voices
which might bring you to yourself at last.

My own voyage deferred
for I must work the loom
and ply the yarn
to finish a fabric
which represents our lie.

Well, I've had it, Odysseus!
I'll weave no more.
I *am* Penelope, I *am* myself.
and push out from your shore.

To the Shadow of Myself

When I stand before lamps of truth
I almost see you
flattening out before me on the ground,
or sidling along a wall – you sneaky thief!

You lack substance,
flirting with every bulb you encounter,
lending your dark dimension to the light.

You draw my best moments into corners,
pummel them with weightless fists
and love to contradict me –

Always impatient for something.

I just can't shake you, shadow.
Even when the light is out
I know you're there, like a stubborn fact.

Oedipus and Electra

You suck my breast, baby –
impossible to wean
but know I will no longer fight
to nourish our phantom dream

I see now what a child you are
how your being there draws from me.
I cannot be your mother –
when I want you to father me.

Red Booth

I sneak into the red booth,
feed some coins into the tarnished slot
spin the dial to hear a voice.

The pale green interior
inscribed with scratched initials
invites me to carve names;
drop the black receiver
cold to ear and hand.

The phone rings
right through to my heart
and goes on ringing.

Where are you wanderer –
Who are you out stalking now?

There's no return.
The slot's silver smile swallows my coins.
I keep my heart down,
its trapped effusion of words,
and turn up my collar against night.

Lonely Women

Feel the moon's gravity in their cells
stretch themselves thin
across an expanse of sheets
seeking that warm shot of skin
remembered for the way it once made them cleave
to breathing flesh and bone.

Mid Drift

Sunday,
in the East End market café –
yiros, Greek salad
olives, feta cheese,
baklava, Turkish coffee.
Together, we eat.

But your eyes feast on lithe legs
passing the wobbly table
of our communion,
drift to bare midriffs –
no two the same.

So much of this is ritual.
Can we only exist together
in spheres of physical language
and fantasy
with green metal expanses between us?

Metal legs rasp on brick floors,
scatter the illusion of our sentences
into the market crowd of legs and navels.

Argument

s/he hurled the African violet
against the wall
and shattered the evening

I don't remember
the argument
just moist black soil
scattered terracotta fragments.

Holiday

I remember
the long passage
and the old black telephone
(for incoming calls only)

I remember
the large bedroom
(three beds and a wardrobe)
with a window looking out
across the barren yard,
stone wall and beach below

I remember the sea
and all his promises

Christmas still on our lips
we wore tinsel in our hair
and summoned the festive spirit.

Stranger

Stranger
you crush me like a wave
pulling me under
you fill my mouth with seaweed
I'm drowning.

Slipping Out

I sit and stare
at the blank surface of his desk;
hear his laugh, in stickers
that peel off the drawers
like curling lips,
or behind me on the bed,
out of the washed laundry of his recent stay.

I imagine my hand
smoothing his crew cut hair –
until I feel it
growing through my fingertips
into the pattern of my print.

His eyes
cast down under the brim of his Nike cap;
the shy smile that runs to his lips
as if there is no tomorrow to speak of.

He's twelve and wants his father now.
His mother the wrong sex,
like the irritation of sisters he leaves behind.

It's *only* another suburb, another world.
Our telephone voices
are all that connect
through unbearable space.

When he was inside me,
I sensed movement –
an invisible butterfly
brushing its wings
on my inside skin.

I spoke to him through walls of skin.
My voice, a vibration in our shared blood;
his bones, moving across my belly like a wave
which breaks
in its own good time.

Now he visits once a fortnight,
for short weekends, which always end
reliving loss.

When I ask if he's happy
he looks at the ground,
not the fault line of my face,
where I struggle with cracks,
and my voice slips through
to say he can always come back.

I contract
with the slow pain of birth;
grip the mask to my face;
gulp the gas of drift –
the separation;
sensation of shoulders slipping out
of me, the dark cavity,
the ache.

His room, an absence
where I sit,
and wish him back.

When I was your mother

I was too soft
my instinct was to cushion
the vulnerability of fontanelle
little pulse
I suckled you
smoothed powder
on bare cheeks
soothed
whispered
rhymes
Now I am dead to you
I was too hard
memories do not hold
words and sentiments
twist in your thoughts
you are heartless
telling me I don't exist
I nurse my own vulnerabilities
prepare to let you go
again, and again.

Ashes

Your great-grandchildren place red carnations
on the polished surface of all that's left of you;
grasp your weight in brass handles,
threaded with scallops of white crepe.

The pastor speaks as if he has known you
all your life, but you were a late immigrant
always clutching at your Welsh roots,
and we send you into the flames with a Gaelic prayer.

Between hymns, he takes the liberty
of slipping in a salvation message.
I want to run from this too hot room, its human silences;
shake off the unbearable light.

Later, you will return to the country of your blood
where my grandfather will shake out your ashes
on the mountainside at Brynithel
where our ancestor climbed from the valley

to marry her beloved
in the thirteenth century chapel;
where family ghosts shadow the earth's veins
in all the mines of the valley
your ashes seep in with the rain.

Ghosts

In the restaurant
we cannot speak for ghosts.
Yesterday's breeze picks at your spine.

From a patch of limestone wall,
a ram's dead yellow eyes
watch out of its severed head.

'Thirty years ago, this building was a ruin
in a field of tall grass,' you say,
smelling pine needles, warm earth, the nearby sea,
you hid there, wagging school,
your eight year old back
tucked against the rough stone wall
where other years, other lives crumbled away.
'There were ghosts then too,' you say
and your eyes are like mist
touching an open field.

Shuttlecock

Turning the fork through a mound of earth
found burnished bone rubbed white.
Fragment of vertebra
from two centuries' burial
disinterred
on this curved hump of hillside.

She turns old bone in flesh of palm;
measures with mind – human or animal.
Over whispers of wheat grass,
calls to her husband
who raises his shovel high
and finger taps the bone
between his eyes.

She hurls a shuttlecock of bone
which he hits against paddock and sky,
down the length of their land,
out of sight, out of mind.

I Killed a Bee

I killed a redback spider
Turned over a garden chair
its fat red stripe
connected with my fear
I felt the tingle of bloodlust
on my tongue.

I killed a redback
now watch for reincarnations
under every seat.

*

I killed a cockroach.
Fear of dirt my alibi
saw it scuttle across mind's eye
from rubbish bin to lip of my glass.

I killed a cockroach.
Disposing of its dark glossy carcass,
I felt almost purified.

*

I killed a bee.
Carried it from the washing line
caught in the collar of my blouse.

Shook it free but fear of its sting
made me reach for the spray.
I watched it struggle with the coat of white poison
and could not undo my thoughtless act.

A beautiful creature
forced to a final clumsy dance

I left the room with my guilt.
Now the taste of honey
is tainted with shame.

Home From the Hunt

Hot –
the smell of him
desert track
winding its red dust
into bleached bush

his hunter's breath
stalking my throat.
Knife of his tongue
carving its silent language
between the rise and fall
of my breasts.

Aphrodisiac armpit –
I lick scent
from its dark cave.
Soft hair of musk
brushes my lip
with its animal heat.

His red dust
in me
the dry grass
scrub of his jaw
grazes
the delta of my cheek
sifts
its sediment of gold.

We kiss –
the warm wet
moistens
our cracked earth loins
flux of muscle
and bone

blood scent
on fingers
traces of flesh
under the nails
the thrill
of the chase
the gunshot
splintering of bone

the knife blade
flushed
under running water
tore into flesh
stripped
the camouflage
of hides
clean off
the glistening meat
the meat
we're hungry for
the flayed carcass
spouting honey –
home from the hunt.

Night Shoot

These men are crazy.
At dusk in the old quarry
under a silk net of rain,
they tinker with flashing lights,
targets and pistols
with precise commitment.

Deep inside army jackets,
felt hats tight over earmuffs,
they plan their course of fire.

When the sky is ink blue over the hills,
it should be dark, silent, still
but these men are electric wires
arcing on wet roads,
they race through makeshift corridors
of old piled tyres,
finger triggers,
draw pistols
and FIRE!

Powder smoke
floats through rain –
I watch amazed.

The Gun

He is the gun
secretly carried
in a shoulder holster
beneath the heavy jacket.
He is all defence
going off half-cocked
at shadows.

He is the gun
that points its accusing barrel at me.
He is protection and fear
with no guarantee.

Cold as steel. Volatile as gunpowder.
He is 'trust me'
with a safety catch
fitted to his trigger-happy hand.

He is the gun
that goes off with a bang;
selects targets
to make victims
in his fixed sights.

He is the gun going off
in the dark of night.

Syrinx

When naked god Pan
(blend of animal and man)
sees lovely Syrinx
by the river
bathing her feet,
chaos and lust rage
in his chest.
He must possess the nymph's serenity,
must touch her tawny breast.

Her contours
lure his flaming eye.
Her stillness
makes his heart race.
He'll pursue the virgin nymph
until she tires of the chase;
claim her with his passion;
conquer serenity;
keep her as a wife.

II

    She takes flight, as Pan pursues.
        Lithe legs swishing
                through long grasses,
            feet tripping on rock and stone,
      she comes to a stream,
            too deep to cross,
                begs the water nymphs
        to change her form.

III

It was her decision.
The sun's fingers –
a kinder penetration,
warming her thoughts
as she lies
on the river bank,
the wind's music
lightly lifting her hair.

Her slender body
becomes reed,
her thoughts enter
the soil like roots.

To be so pure
and weightless;
to let the mind drift
like a leaf
on the water's surface;
to exist
in a single moment;
to be free.

IV

Pan thinks he has his will,
makes of her an instrument,
to transform
by the act of union,
with his lips.
The wind plays its music
through her.
She is melody.

Zen and the Art of Cleaning

I enter
your space –
its detachment.
What is, *is*.
Simplicity
of surfaces.
No ornament,
utensil
or pretence.
The string mop glides
on polished boards.
Your bedroom –
uncluttered –
foam mattress, feather quilt
a single sheet
placed carefully,
a few books
on the art
of being.
I sift
live dust
in endless blue
of window,
ocean.

Lava and Rain

the lava sun burns and runs
concrete is volcanic ash

there's a fire
and the sprinklers
are on heat

in the shade-house,
green corrugations distil light
to feeble shadow

a honeyeater drips
from the shade cloth sky
to steal a drink

I lie naked on a sofa bed
that's drawn its own heat
compete with silent monstera leaves

catch the drift of liquid mist
the fragile cool
of fine green rain.

The Street at Five a.m.

Being in the street at five a.m.
is like lifting the latch
on the tedium of enclosure
or letting a dog loose on the beach.
Not yet a place of daylight
where everything that happens is too real,
it is a place of shadows and half-light
where possibility plays in hidden shapes.
A scale of scents weaves spring air
with the potent warmth of jasmine
cross-weave of damp earth, snail slime
leaf rot, lavender and bird droppings.
You might stand in a state of awe
and stare at the ghost-moon taking its leave
or throw your arms wide
breathing deeply, as all around you neighbours sleep.
The street at five a.m. is at peace
it could almost be paradise
as the sky yields gold ribbons of light in the east
bruised purple shifts slowly to lilac-blue.
And none but you to breathe its promise.

The River

At dusk, follow a track by the river
until you reach a channel,
dividing the bank, where lit windows
of island houses flicker
like a shoal of candles, beneath water
and you can go no further.

Then, stand a while, in the mauve light, breathing.
And as you breathe out, forgetting the day,
something unfolds itself
like a wing spanning great distance –
flies out to meet the sounds of evening
symphony of insects tuning strings.

You become the air and the music,
the mauve light and the candles.
The raft beneath your feet no longer grass,
nor even earth, but something finer.
Though the bank is broken,
the path sheer down to dark and shining water,
you've travelled great distance –
the river unwinds before you.

Hawkesbury River Visit

I – The Dream

A long-held dream of mine to visit the Hawkesbury
a quaint timber shack right on the river
so close you can hear the lap of water night and day
rhythmic knock of wooden boat
moored at the jetty
feel the turning tides through rustic floor boards
a large window taking in the view
forested hills, hazed blue
wide expanse of river
oyster racks just breaking the surface
book-lined walls and a nook for reading
a window seat with plump cushions
river birds wading at water's edge
graceful bending to beak the shallows
snap and swallow fish, pelicans gliding
just a stone's throw from Robert and Juno
following the same moon, rising above trees
framed in a picture window
afternoon tea in a garden, overlooking the jetty
literary conversations and river music
perhaps take the boat out to explore the flow of the river
see the sights along the shores
closer to islands.

I – The Reality

There is no doubt of its beauty.
We catch glimpses of the river
as the GPS guides us to Cheero Point
but we are dead beat after the long journey
keen to put up our feet and make a fresh pot of tea.
We only have one night
not likely we'll have time to explore.
First thing in the morning we must hit the road again.
I'm disappointed.
Our river shack sits on a narrow lane overlooking the river
there's a pontoon and private jetty
cordoned off with orange bunting
recent rains have collapsed the verges
no access to dip hands and toes in water
I long for that connection, to know the river's flow
feel its current course through me.
Our city car is too large to reverse into the garage
gouged from stone, under the living quarters
but a kindly neighbour allows us to park
further up the lane where it widens
we carry our belongings the distance
then up the river stone stairs.
The living space is compact and modern
with a tiny balconet to tease us outdoors
I am grateful for that much.

Sidling into the slender space
    to breathe in
        the
        coming
        night
        to
        listen
        i
        m
        a
        g
        i
        n
        e
        the
        joy
        of
        spending
        a
        lifetime
        here.

River bend

When the tide is low
and the sun doesn't shine
the river bend blends
into bleached scrub
but you know
it's always there
waiting for the rush
of high tide

Room

In a corner of the room,
in an oriental vase,
dead branches
sprayed with artificial silver
beckon like witches' fingers.

Before an open fireplace,
two Persian cats sprawl
on a shag-pile rug –
omnipotent gods,
indifferent to sparks.

Tutankhamen's mask
watches from the mantel.
Its worthless gold
filches the firelight
from various reflections.
A framed mirror above the soft white couch,
luminous black piano
against the wall.

She is practising magic.
I know the Tarot burns beneath
a silk scarf on the table's glass surface,
with a trillion configurations of future.

When it is time
for me to leave her
satisfied as a gorged cat
she'll give me a cue –
standing to check her hair
in the looking glass.

Hardly aware of me or my wondering
that her mask has slipped,
revealing the ashes of her lust.

The Shy Girl

The shy girl enters the room but never the crowd
lingers near walls, invisible as the wind
words form on her lips
but she never says them aloud
such a chore to leave the house or get out of the car
like a flare off the shore, her signals of distress
seem to draw every eye
the attention leaves her raw

The shy girl is always alone, but yearns for friendship
deeper and more tangible than online social networks
where writing on walls flows more smoothly than conversation,
and the keyboard voices her thoughts.

The room is full of people she knows, but none of them really know her.
She should say hello, though she's afraid they won't remember
…her name…or where and when they last met…or that they'll disconnect.

She tries to see that others have vulnerabilities,
…uncertainties…insecurities
that they too tremble and trip on words
wonders how to move beyond pleasantries
without overstepping imperceptible lines.
She looks for quick exits and ladies loos – there's safety in cubicles.

She'll take her seat too early and fumble with the programme,
clean her glasses, remove non-existent stones from her shoes,
then leave as the audience is applauding, ahead of the crowd.

She wishes that confidence would magically descend
and let her mingle smoothly.
But it's always the same.
She enters the room, never the crowd.
Words scatter and scrape in her brain.
Her palms tick with beads of fear, and
she exits quickly from the reality of social networks.

Dear Professor

I've never been to the Bronx,
or crossed Manhattan in a cab
but I feel the elation
on the cabby's face
as he offers to cut your fare
for the glory of a rare ride
with *true* Bronx blood.

I enter your mother's kitchen,
(its discovery of Italian scents)
where I am clothed
in the novel of your life
the careless stains of a dreamer
blotching my dress. Italian sauces
falling in red suns of worship
onto the pages of a borrowed book –
Light in August – your mother's voice
trying to reach you, and haul you back
from creations of mind

and later, your grandmother's question,
'What kind of a doctor *are* you ?'
finding you one that 'can't cure'.

Had I been in America in the 60s,
and a student of yours,
I might've fallen at your feet
or torn a leaf of passion from your book
between the covers of a motel bed
and licked the neon flashes from your skin.
Ah yes! I would be drawn to drunkenness and sin,
and whisper wicked phrases in your ear.

I watch your lips quiver,
sense your emotion,
grapple with desire.

Want

I want
   to hang on your lip
like that cigarette
   you just rolled
   and set alight
   the way you drew
        hard
          as if life, or death,
      depended on it
   dragged its smoke
   down into your chest
let it escape
…satisfied…
from your throat.

      I want
to be that rich tobacco
   when you can't resist
      its open pouch
      must thrust
      your nose in
for the aroma it exudes.
   I want
   to know that artistry
   of thumb and finger
that passionate restraint
the long lick
   of preparation.

I want
   to burn
       my insides to ash
          in your embrace.

  And when
I have entered your body
       disguised
         as your breath
       I want
       to rise again
   with that next cigarette
fire up in your fingers
   the slow burn of addiction
making us want
and want   and want.

I want to kiss you

I want to kiss you on your lips
while looking deep into your eyes
and find myself there in your soul
I want to rest my head on your bare chest
kiss your nipples as you stroke my hair
and feel forever safe
I want to know the pleasure of your tongue
as our endorphins flow together like molten chocolate
I want to eat with you the delight of contentment
in violet hours in a soft bed
I want to go back to a time of youth
and know each other inside out
I want to ride the ups and downs with you
while exploring the fairground
know the security of your arms
in the darkness of ghost train tunnels
I want it to be OK and be forever
I want to give and take
drift on a raft of love
in the deepening lake
I want to open myself to you
and be blessed with your touch
remind me what it is to make love
remind me what it is to feel a lover's kiss
to be the object of desire
but be kind to me and love me in return
let us hold each other through many nights

Rock

My tongue reads your nipples like Braille.
Savours salt, honey, musk
in its narration of skin.

I lick at your eyelids.
They are smooth pebbles worn from rock
beat with the pulse of rock and tide.

I watch you ride the pleasure waves
your mouth agape in ecstasy

I want to climb
inside the dark of your body
and like a cave dweller
inscribe your walls
with my essence

To chip away rock
expose tunnels of tenderness
to crawl along our heightened senses
in a mutual penetration
of hard exteriors.

When you hold me

When you hold me close to your body
something beyond the warmth of flesh
moves in me, sparking each cell
with the delight of contentment

When you make love to me
and your eyes suddenly open to meet my own
I feel the connection as a warm lake in my belly
spreading ripples
up into my chest, heart, throat, temples

I lose all my boundaries
in this new dimension of us
as though I could float free of my body
and meld with the gentle aspect of your being.

Sunday Morning

We nestle in warm
moulds of skin
listening to steady rain.

I turn to touch the shadows
of your face –
light leaps through me

We are the gentle pleasure
of sunshine after rain.

Google Earth

At the time of devastation in New Orleans following a hurricane (2005)

That night
we swept across
Rio de Janeiro
in search of
Christ the Redeemer

and in the morning,
with the rain,
some local evangelists came;
our roof leaked tears
into an empty cup.

Inter Section (A Dream)

They have come here before me
along avenues of riotous light.
I sense them
in pools of water, rippled neon,
their chameleon reflections drown mine.

My many faces fuse black and yellow
only soft rain on my hair reminds me I am real.
In thunderous tones, I deny the tempo
of their schismatic beat
and pull tight the lining of my cloak.

Their shadows rage in shuddering tree-tops.
Everything speaks of them.
The wind, hoarse with its blasphemies;
the stagnant desire of a red car
stalled at an intersection;
the brutal lights, and windows open to rain.

I hesitate on an arc of intuition
and sense their invasion of breathing –
like the subtle penetration of rain.

Dream

If I could paint my dream
I'd paint me naked,
descending the canvas,
the crescent steps of moonshine,
into a Roman bath,
or an indoor pool,
with a central fountain.

I'd paint my long hair flowing into water;
the fluid motion of hips and buttocks
easing into clear liquid
like a vision of something
seen through blue glass.

I'd brush the gentle limbs
of the blonde child
wading through me,
and reveal the white wall
opening as a door

where a well-groomed woman
stands and gestures
while I marvel at the articulation of her request.

She calls for a simple tissue
but the journey is everything –
I must swim the deep waters
and delve into the box of terrors
with its dark corners,
its ferocious guards.

The soft pink tissue unfolds in my palm like a lotus
but retains its exquisite shape.
I must carry it above the waters
to prevent disintegration
and deliver it whole.

If I fail, I might lose sight
of the young girl
and the woman.

When I succeed, I will know the right perspective
and *live* the vibrant self of my dream.

Scars

Scars are the post-it notes of pain
they remember and remind us
each little hurt flutters and inflames
spells out initials carved in skin
revives the bitterness of shame
traces soft silver furrows
of pregnancy's slow stretch
holds the pattern of knitted flesh
against lacerations of memory.

Some scars are kept hidden
others proudly displayed.
Still, scars mar, blemish, disfigure and deface
speak of names and symbols
sliced or lasered from the skin of ankles, arms, wrists.

Scars are signs of trespass
of accidental wounds, deliberate slashes
episiotomies, surgery
love, loss.

A scar is an emblem of healing
we are the initiates of our scarring.
Scarred tissue is said to be stronger
and scars make us human
they enter us invisibly
never only skin deep.

Only Thirty

I am only thirty.
What have I accomplished?
a marriage – dissolved as a pill on the tongue
two children – I cannot think of leaving
learning, as I must,
there will not be nine lives for me
– I am no cat
more a moth
that has met its flame
not nine lives, or even one
and nothing to blame.

Air – a precious commodity –
will perish in my lung
diagnosis:
my wings burn behind me
my body a black mass
ice crystals form in my veins.
I am only thirty.
I will die
or I will rise again.

The tumbling dice will number my days;
with the right parts I could have a chance.
Lady Lazarus, show me your hand.

The Search

The search beam sweeps
its blade of light
across a dark hill

scores a path
edge sharp
swings back
to bleach the garden
of shadows

reveal us as watchers
binoculars trained
on the movement of light
the jagged line of searchers crossing
the hill with dim torches

when police come knocking
to search neighbourhood gardens
we learn about the autistic boy
who scaled a gate and vanished

convoys of cars trawl the street
and park in cul-de-sacs by the river
the helicopter touches down
menacingly near water

it is all too real now
the hours run on adrenaline
binoculars are useless

the helicopter, finding nothing,
rises from wetlands
and curves back over suburbs

A hot night,
we cannot sleep for thinking.
The drone of rotor blades
promises nothing.

Morning brings an end to the year
but a fresh chopper circles
too bright and noisy for daybreak
and a news crew sets up on the hillside.

The helicopter hovers
over a large pond, fringed with reeds
where pelicans glide and fishers gather

his small body
is pulled gently from the water
the news crew packs up
the tall reeds whisper

the end of a year,
is marked, inappropriately, by fireworks
on the horizon at midnight.

The Weir

Generations of Adelaide boys
fished and swam at the Torrens Weir.
There's a photo at the State Library
of five boys playing in shallow water
on the other side of the sluice gates
before they were installed.
It's taken in the early 1900s
and all the boys are naked,
without any shame.
Was it different then?
Or did the men with secret desires
always lurk there in bushes and change sheds
awaiting their prey.

One summer I was taken by surprise
in the old stone building, cool and damp
reeking of urine and keeping the shouts of play
at a distance.

Paralysed, I clenched my whole body, aware of my skin
the tug at my swim trunks. Thick fingers trembling
over early pubic hair. The fight or flight response letting me
    down
as bearded lips brushed me there, thrill of tongue, trembling
    thighs
a sick chill in my stomach, being drawn in, afraid, confused,
    but
somehow pleasant, heart lurching, unsure how to move away,
to end.

Sudden creak of old wooden door, the slackening of a spider web,
a fly caught in sticky silk, to be devoured. The world of boys burst in,
innocent, the flick of towels, push and shove of rough play, breaking
the act, in a flurry of escape. Utterly changed.

Relief

I

All week, like the worst migraine pumping to shatter the
 bounds of skull,
rolling from hemisphere to hemisphere in airless rooms of
 twisted sheets
they long for relief from the sleep-snatching crematorium of
 night.

The oscillating fan, diminished by its own squeak,
leaks oil on the dresser – blood, sweat, and tears
seep into the loaded dark.

Sirens drill out the cores of dreams
like brain surgeons exploring the neuroblast of flame
exploding tree trunks in the mythic bush
fire of no respite, sweat bastes the body on its spit.

II

Rain, in slow fat drops, seems pregnant with the foetus of
 relief,
too late for withered marigolds, but they will it to grow
from immaculate cloud-conception
to sky-splitting saviour rain.

Everything cries out for it with throat-swollen thirst
the asphyxiated plants, the penury of earth
and rooftops welcome the tune of its birth
drumming the death of heat.

III

It's Sunday and finally cool.
the washing machine, flat out with its revolution
of making a clean break
sends the pipes into violent judders
and suds, like remnants of energy, thin in the stainless steel
 sink.

Miss Wiley Visits Springwood (1918)

1

Glorious morning.
Sunlight makes the gum trees new.
So peaceful, leaving the city.
Only the train rocking along its tracks
toward the Blue Mountains.

The novel, unread, open on my lap;
my city gaze drawn out through windows
to a silence of trees and sky –
awed at such beauty.

Two hours later, I arrive in another world
where the hiss and squeal of brakes
wakes me from a dream, still three miles from the Lindsay's
the only horse and buggy travelling another way.

Perhaps I will walk in trees and sunlight
along dirt tracks – rainbow birds swooping before me
flashes of colour whirled on a palette.

But my errand awaits, there is no time to wander.
The parcel grows heavy in my hand.
There's a motor car, I'm told – the only one in town
for a fee, its owner might run me out.

When I tap at the office window, the estate agent, reluctant,
tells me Lindsay's buggy might soon arrive – I ought to wait.

The Lindsay's buggy will not come, I know,
for I am not expected – an invitation might have been denied.
Better to arrive on the veranda, to stand among the nudes,
unshockable as I am, and plead 200 autographs from his hand.

For six shillings, I strike a bargain.
The agent is curious, but my gaze drawn again through windows.
I map, by heart, the landscape as we go.

This is where it begins

in a dry creek bed
strewn with litter
the inviting dark
a mystery to follow.
You can go so far
before you feel
the compressed
rumble
the closing in
of otherworlds
the forgotten weather
under the city streets
beneath the traffic
with your metal torch
illuminating scrawls
the rubble stubbing
shining wet in thin beamed
light
it might be raining now
dry creeks filling
cracks seeping
dripping pipes
you follow the curved bricks
into subterranean grottoes
climbing rusted rungs
to other openings
wary of small movements
scuttling of odd beings
bent almost double
in the concrete veins

of your city
seeking its heart
its peculiar blend
of safety and danger.
You know you shouldn't
have come alone
but it was impulse
one step led to another
and you pray that your batteries
don't go flat
that you aren't caught by
a torrent of water
that you can find a way out through
a grate
or a gutter
that a plate
doesn't open
onto a busy intersection.
It's unlikely there's another
creek bed at the end of the tunnel
you could die down here
while life goes on, oblivious,
above
but you're a kid
with a curious mind
wanting to know Adelaide's secrets
what's at her core.

At home with the fetid sludge
the possibility of a dead body,
of giant rats
and the panic
rising
until you find a way
to set yourself free
pushing up on a last century grate
squinting at bleached light
as you squeeze through a drain's mouth
into the bustle of human traffic
the mechanics of noise
stink of sewer
imbued in the fabric of your clothes
happy to have come through
and traversed the underground network
upon which your city is built
understanding
a little better now
that there is more to this place
than can be seen on the surface.

Something Like Egypt

A week or so after our arrival
I'm driving with my father
in a borrowed FJ Holden
down Port Road to see the wharves
his large hands guiding the wheel
shirt sleeves rolled to his elbows
thinly rolled cigarette pasted to his lip.

It seems a hot day, though still winter
sun heating the painted dashboard
red leather scent fusing this moment to memory
row upon row of palm trees
planted on the wide median strip
convincing me we now belong
to an exotic and tropical country
something like Egypt.

The Pug Hole

From Port Road, Welland, to the brickworks
at Hindmarsh, was only a three k bike ride.

Off the main road, just beyond the river
the pug hole was an adventure playground,
where we'd spend all day clambering down
into the cocoon of clay, with deep pockets
of water, sprouting reeds, and a cache of
rusted rotting junk we transformed for play.
Old corroded tins we threaded with wire
for catching tadpoles in murky puddles.

Abandoned car bodies, afloat in deep
wells of oily water, became pirate ships
as we straddled them, and fought each other
with sticks, constantly shifting our weight
to keep the wrecks from sinking into the mire.

It wasn't unusual then for a boy
to carry a slug gun or .22, slung across his back,
to fire at bottles or tins lined up at a distance.

There were holes all over Hindmarsh and Brompton
which, having given up their clay for bricks
became dumping grounds for waste
a rich source of amusement
for children's imaginations.

The watery fissures were muddy but slicked
with slippery rainbows. When you stopped to notice,
the smell was a mixture of dead animal, iron and rotten socks.

When it was time to ride back home
we carried the swampy scent of the pug hole
on our clothes,
to our mothers' ire and disgust.

All Roads Lead to Bombala

We should've filled up in Cooma
took a right turn across yellow Monaro plains
under steel-grey skies, less than 40 ks to Nimmitabel.

When we arrived, there was no pump in town
the tank was on empty, fuel alert beeping.
Locals sprawled on steps outside the pub
confirmed 'No petrol in Nimmi'
pointed north-west to Bombala
a long way from Bega.

We had no other option – it was Bombala or bust.
The light slowly dwindling
we had visions of sleeping on the roadside
or walking through shadowy scrub
with a tin can.

With the car in neutral
we were grateful
for every downhill
s t r e t c h
arrived in Bombala
with barely a drop in the tank.

We were tired of the road now
and Bega seemed a long way back.
Though we didn't much like Bombala,
and Bombala didn't like us,
it had a thriving truckers' motel
and a receptionist who gave us strangers the evil eye
we almost stayed, but there were queues
as trucks rolled in and the phone rang crazily
telling us there was no room
we'd be driving back
to meet the Snowy Mountains Highway
ride the bends all the way down to Bega
a hundred clicks away.

We thought we'd seen the back of Bombala
but next morning, as we said goodbye to Bega
headed for the east coast, and Eden,
even as we headed inland,
west along the Princes Highway
every second turn-off had a green and white sign
with bold letters
proudly displaying the distance to Bombala.

To Lake Pedder

I've only seen your image on a screen.
A wash of muted colours
pinks and greens.
Your lights and shadows
apportioned to a frame.
Your history
abbreviated to captions:
Melaleucas bent and weathered
on your southern shore.
Mount Solitary, caught
in a golden hourglass,
fringed with leaves at dawn.

I'd like to know you
without their hydro electric harness
reining you in and riding you down
the depths of flood
until you drown drown drown.
I'd like you untouched and natural
below the Sentinel Range,
silent and spiritual,
like the unicorn
wild and free.

Violet Town

Violet Town
The slow shift of clouds.

Barely a sound on this hot afternoon.
You could strum a guitar to an audience of none
in the main street under leaves in dappled light.
So quiet you can hear the distant approach
of a V-Line train long before the clang of crossing bells.

Such a pretty name on Honeysuckle Creek
once known as Violet Ponds
where streets are flower-named
an easy wind makes old branches creak
seed pods clatter onto tin roofs.

There's a weir somewhere, we've heard
but this is just a comfort stop off the Hume
en route from Euroa to Benalla
almost a mark on the Kelly Trail
famous only for its markets
hand-painted saws, home-made jams and Killing Heidi.

The inspiration for poems and songs
Violet Town – the slow shift of clouds
ingenious teens devising their own fun
summer days dreaming of oceans
as footpaths blister and crack
where silence is solid.

You can strum a guitar to an audience of none
in the main street under leaves in dappled light
so quiet you can hear the distant approach of a V-Line train
long before the clang of crossing bells.

Passing through the Suez Canal

People say there isn't much to see
along the shoreline of the Suez Canal
but I don't think they were looking.
Peering over the deck rail
I saw the desert sands shifting
sunken ships that might block our passage
through the expanse of bisque and blue.
Only three years since the crisis
I could feel the eyes of troops upon us
I'm sure I saw a soldier or two with rifles
slung over their shoulders, and I know there were tanks
glinting darkly in afternoon sun.
Here and there were patches of lush green
little oases in a parched land
an obelisk of petrified sand
its shadow pointing to the calm surface
a convoy of colourful cargo boats
wings of white sea birds.
A mirage of pyramids
shimmering in the distance.

Crossing the Equator

It was mayhem when we crossed the equator
I didn't know what to expect
so I hid behind a bench on deck
and peered through slats
to watch old Neptune march around the pool
his long white hair gleaming
like seaweed, his silver trident catching the sun.
Many of the passengers wore their clothes
inside out, but some were looking sheepish.
It was ambivalent fun, tainted with threat.
Somebody said we would be thrown overboard
into the swirling ocean, protected
against sharks and drowning. I trembled behind
the bench as a man in trunks was caught
in a cascade of cold spaghetti and a cloud
of flour dust drifted down from above
settling on heads and shoulders.

After a while, my mother coaxed me out to join the party.
Exposed, I was a target catching my own drift
of flour dust then, scooped up roughly, I was thrown
into the baptismal pool to qualify for a certificate.
It wasn't so bad, my fear was born of uncertainty
but now I was one of them.

There was a dust storm when we crossed the equator
a thick red veil as far as I could see. I'm sure we had to alter course
and cross back over. Neptune didn't make a second appearance
he gave up his costume and became one of the crew.
When the celebrations were over and most of the passengers
back in their cabins, I sat alone on the bench that had hidden me
listening to an eerie silence, watching the red sky darken
wondering about the new world we were soon to enter.

A Tourist in Te Aroha

New Zealand 1999

I stand, with my camera poised, in the busy street
gazing up at Mount Te Aroha, mountain of love,
at the way it wears this morning's sun –
a crown of rays, ferried down
shadowed slopes in haze of light.

I can't capture on film the hazy beam
that stirs warm trickles of joy
through solar plexus, swirls to fingertips,
floods me with a sense of home
as though my blood had known its myth.

I am only a tourist passing through.
The road is a thief
stealing me for its false pilgrimage
when everything whispers 'stay',
and I long to reach the summit of such love.

Fish

Blue face

    beneath the water
        mouthing stars

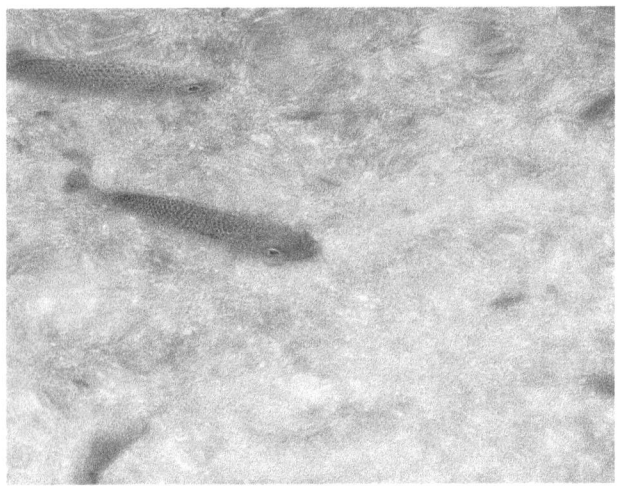

Night Meditation

…body slides
between crisp sheets
of cool, clean cotton

wears the soft weight
of feathers like a new skin

eyes relax, close
on ceiling shadows
pale light
through parted curtains

I practise falling
into imagined clouds

as day thoughts drift
across mind sky

a breeze rattles the window
a mosquito tunes its violin
my husband breathes
beside me

Big Sky

'Big sky' she exclaimed on arriving
I didn't need to look up
it was imprinted in my mind
with its frequent double rainbows
shifting colours
through winter storm to summer fine

Bruised indigo to salmon pink
every hue between
grey, apricot, cobalt, powder blue.
Sometimes Zen empty
or smoky orange warning of scrub fire.

I've tracked jets and planes across its space
watched clouds descend on hillsides
turning dark and broody
or lighting up gold from within
their thunderous music
spectacular with lightning.

A playground for wetland birds
flying in formation, heading off toward ocean
Graceful pelicans gliding on thermals
light aircraft coming in to land across the river.

One New Year's Eve,
that blue and yellow helicopter
hovering above pond and reeds
in search of a missing child

The sky is never still
over the wetlands
it is open but also holds its secrets
like the trillion stars that emerge at night
there is always more to know
oh Secret Sky, there is so much to celebrate.

Guitar

I have the body of a guitar.
When I lie down to meditate
my neck is straight
I clear my mind
of things I've fretted about
let go my strings of attachment.

My soul is a sound box
it draws in the songs of birds,
pulsation of insects,
gentle movement of breezes,
transforms the vibrations of nature
into meditation music.

I breathe in
breathe out
repeat the cycle
creating chords of calm
to lift me above the physical
resonating with riffs of bliss
tuned to perfection.

Orange

You dig your thumbs into the peeled orange,
split delicate crescents veined with pith.

Pull white strings of silence
along grooves in the membrane.

Bite the sweet suck; trail of juice on your chin.
Tatters of flesh on our best crockery.

Baptism

She could not imagine there was a heaven.
It was nothing she could hold in her vision
and climb to through dreams.
She could not trust the untouchable
the reality she could never know.

There were only loose threads of past and present
she twisted on stretched-out fingers
to weave into days she could touch and feel;
voices in the tortuous void, that did not resemble speech;
faceless, nameless sounds she must resist like early death.
They came too soon, so that she did not hear
only listened to the confusion she felt.

In the room of invisible faces she must walk alone
and feel their eyes upon her, knowing they could see her desire
like the full-blown rose dropping its garments
knowing she would fall into the arms of a stranger
and wake to discover she had given too much of her self.

She remembered the harvest festivals of her childhood,
the palm leaves they wove into crosses,
the stained glass window.
She could press her eye into a red segment
and imagine heaven looked that way.
When she remembered this she did not cry
but went on calmly, tending the soil, weeding the flower bed,
kissing the faces her children held forward to be blessed.
But she could not respond, nor imagine herself intangible as air.

Then, walking in the garden, she met a man,
not a stranger, but clothed in shadows
and she stood in the clear light trembling –
it was enough for her. It was enough.
Until she found that her hands could not stroke his golden skin
for they were unclean, she had murdered love
her tears where they fell on his grave
became tendrils of ivy, twisting out of the soil
to cover the damp mound she felt warm beneath her body.
Was this the false prophet she had buried?
She could not know for it could not be known
but the voices, more clearly defined now,
slowly became a single sound,
a soft bell-like whisper, she felt beneath her skin.
It was in her, leading her on.

She imagined wide plains edging toward desert.
Her senses could fill that space, all heat and airy light.
She could gather up a silence and hold it to her breast.
It did not matter that she was thirsty,
that her feet were blistered. She felt no pain.
The fiery sand beneath her was water –
the chaste and holy water for which she had thirsted.
It surrounded her. She let it flow through her,
surrendered to this new baptism
like a ripple, the heart beat of water,
had wanted this without knowing it was this she craved.

Her new face drank the sun's gold and her hair caught the stars.
She felt a universe inside her. The moon at her feet gathered
the white robe and silvered the path ahead.

It was this she had wanted –
to stand between heaven and earth
and give birth to herself.

My Mother's Voice

She is the soothing tone of her voice
smoothing bedclothes with hands
which are never still
and when she sits
her fingers slip yarn around a needle
and knit the evenings into garments
as her voice dances its bee dance
round the honeycomb of rooms
carrying trays of light snacks
wiping dust from surfaces
until they gleam like unmarked windows.

When she senses danger in a raised voice
she licks its anger like a wound
and coaxes it to heal
for she is the peacemaker
and her voice goes on
breaking into song –
is the harmony of wind
which rocks our family tree
in her cradle of arms
that never breaks.

There's a Strange Bird

There's a strange bird
on the balcony –
one I can't find in the book.
Look – pure white
resembling a dove.
The yin yang
of a black tail spot
overlaid with white feathers.
I thought perhaps
an albino magpie
but for its pink legs
and its silence
and the magpies
chasing it across sky
in dogfight flight.
I guess it's an outcast
seeking sanctuary
in this high place.
When I peer through the window,
its inky eye observes me
and I feel a connection.

Sheoak Guide

You were my guide
through the fallen limbs
and whisperings of the sheoak grove,
pointing out wild mulberry;
slashing thick webs with a split branch;
casting an eye over needles and rocks
for resting snakes.

Though you led me down into gullies
onto gull spattered rocks
I was never afraid.
My shoes, slipping from invisible footholds,
edged along narrow ledges
of warm, glittering slabs,
and you – always there.

Sometimes, you would see things in shadow –
nesting penguins wedged into cracks;
a wallaby dancing in shallow caves;
my cool black stone of pain.

Beside us, clear depths of ocean stirred
and lapped us with spray.
Silence, lacing our minds.
Unspoken words, written on sea.
You held my hand across distances
and taught me to leap.

When rocks broke open to sand,
I sang in clearer voice.
The bay curved before us.
We followed its pristine bow
of white and emerald into sky.

Surreal

Moana Beach

Born from the ocean's dark bed
I am sea creature
slipped out of shell
for this moment's sky –
mother-of-pearl
swirled in orange light
amid the dying blue
and surreal bright moon
full, in boughs
of Norfolk pine.

Beach

Moana

Prone beneath the setting sun
my body spans infinite grains.
The universe in each
enters skin and blood.
I become the beach,
last streak of light
and lapping wave.

Animal…Universe

Kangaroo Island

It's raining
on the island
cut loose
from mainland –
drift into
hot rain
scents of bush
earth, eucalypt

I squat
in autumn evening
alert
animal
senses swivelling
meld with dirt
scrub
sky
star
universe.

Backwards

Unwind, unwind
to the slow
rippled wash
of the morning tide
let go
of it all
let it go
with the slide
of the sea
on hard sand

begin to feel
the sun's warm hand
begin to feel
from the centre out
spirals of light
let them in
to the dark spaces
let them in

let them touch
the memories of this place
our hands
touching briefly
as if
it all happened
and the slowing
of my heart beat
traced our footprints
on this beach
backwards
slowly
backwards

A Voice in the Night

I wake in the night to a soft voice calling
slowly shed my garments of sleep.
Drawn to the garden, along a dark passage
I draw back the curtain to mystical light.

In luminous moonlight, fine rain is falling.
Naked, I kneel on the lawn – wet and silvered –
raise my eyes to flooding white.

I am the moon's bride
waiting in celestial chambers.
I am many points of fusing light;
parts of me tremble
in the moon's ring of rain.

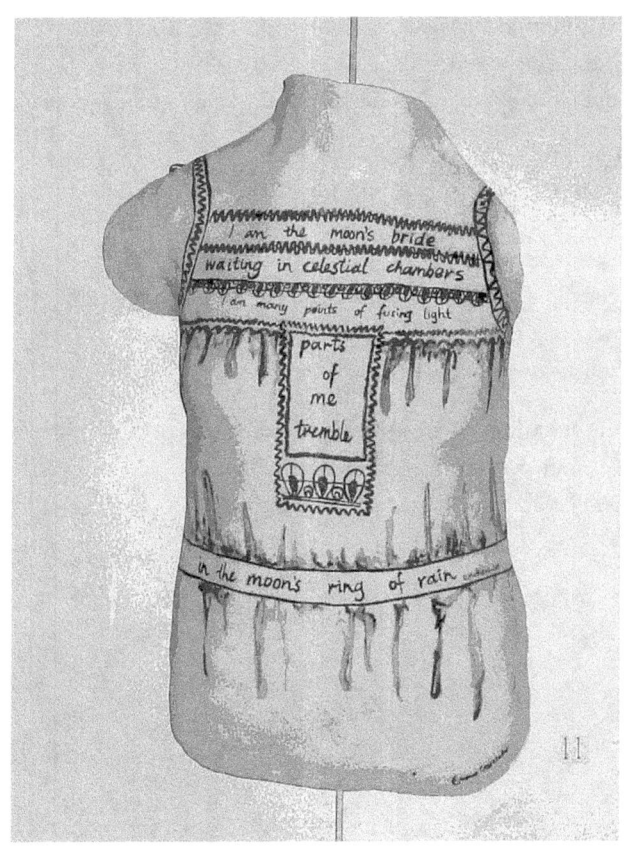

The W(h)ishing of Rain

This morning, while it was still dark,
I rose from a restless dream
and sat in our lounge room, under the lamp, reading Hesse.

Outside, as darkness dimmed
I felt the light and heard the whishing of rain
willing me out of my seat.

For a long time I stood, nose pressed to cool glass,
watching raindrops fall from the veranda
and splash onto the gate.

Then, back in time I went with the whishing of rain
to another morning of freshness and love
and became, for a moment, a child again.

Outside Language

Sometimes
language is insufficient
to capture, to convey
simple beauty

all it offers is cliché
morning dew
diamonds
caught in the spongy raft
of duckweed covering a pond

caught there
and catching
light
nature's jewels
simply
outside language.

Water in a Blue Bowl

Crouching in the garden as a child
I'd lose myself in play, be it water or earth
or, later, the forbidden allure of fire,
was blissful and unaware of time.

Sunlight crinkling water in a blue bowl
I'd ladle it and watch it fall in miniature cascades
then soak a sponge with its weight
and squeeze its rivulets over legs and arms
releasing smeared earth from skin.

Lying face down on grass beneath the apple tree
revealed another world of new green shoots
crumbled earth rims around ant holes
segmented pink-grey worms churning the surface
scents of lawn and leaves and ripening fruits.

Winter Garden Meditation

Sparrows play in the bare branches
of the nectarine tree
a frog calls
from the dietes and wild iris
mulberry leaves fall
with each outward breath of the wind
sunlight and shadow
flirt over shining pond water
I am sparrows dancing
on dark branches
against the blue of a winter sky
I am the frog playing hide and seek
down at the damp root in secret shadow
I am faded leaves floating
to earth on the wind's breath
sunlight and shadow
on lily pads
water reflecting bare branches, winter sky.

Butterfly and bird – two haiku

A white butterfly
at the lip of blue flowers
still as passing clouds

On the plum tree branch
the freed bird steadies itself
uncertain of sky

A Poet's Self-defence

I am NOT the 'I' in these poems.

I am not the 'I' who might use crude language,
or fail to dot my 'I's
I am not the 'she', or the 'he'
and have no paranoid illusions regarding 'they'.

I am NOT the 'I' who pines for lost lovers
nor the 'I' who walks out naked into the moonlight.
I am not the 'I' who cries out in rage
or the one gone insane
to the drip drop of thoughts on a page.

I am not the chain smoker of metaphors, condoning bad habits.
I do not take drugs, or hang out with thugs on city streets.
I am also not the one pathetically sweet
or the 'I' with a voracious sexual appetite.

I do not have a fetish for guns or fast cars.
I am not necessarily the anorexic 'I' with the starving poet fantasy
the unwritten novel, the uncontrollable kids
the ex-lover, or the huge debt.

I am not the 'I' in these poems.
I am merely a figure of speech
a voice in a poem – the unwritten 'I' who writes.

Dandelion Tea

The house smells of jasmine.
Bed sheets dry in sunshine.
The first draft of a new poem finished.
All the lawnmowers in the neighbourhood are whirring.

A cup of dandelion tea,
forgotten, has gone cold
I post to Facebook.

John says, 'The post reads like a poem.
It has the feel of haiku.
Disconnected observations
with gaps your mind can fill.'
Alice hits the nail on the head
'All is right with the world –
all you need is a new cup of tea!'

The kettle boils
I pour steaming water
onto leaves.

Statice

They rise above bitumen
and almost fill a frame of glass.
Bonsai forests: rootless, in purple,
and labial explosions of green;
where constellations of white birds roost
strip them slowly to purple ash.

The Swing

The swing is a musical instrument.
The sound of a badly played violin
when bow grates across strings.
It sings rhythm and rust.
A violin with seats and room for standing.
It draws the shrieks of children's voices
through the blue score of the sky.
It is a concert of discords
with its creaks and screams
that counterpoint the tune –
but always the
  rhy-thm
       rhy-thm
         rhy-thm

Love Poetry

All my life I've loved poetry.
I've sat up at night with it
coaxing rhythms from unruly stanzas,
arranging words and images on a page.

My life was never a blank slate
as my emotions chalked up
poem after poem, from feelings impossible to erase.
An indelible blackboard I wouldn't want the class to see.
Especially once published
when the poems no longer seemed part of me.

Sometimes poetry was suicidal
and I'd love it to death.
Forget your death-of-the-author theories.
It was simply euthanasia of the text.

I loved poetry when I slept alone in my bed.
It was a kind of comfort waking at first light
to find Shakespeare's spine pressed against my cheek,
or Eliot propped up on my pillow
with his band of Hollow Men,
and one or two contemporary poets tangled in my sheets.

I've loved love poetry, death poetry, erotic poetry,
in any shape or form. Real, Surreal, or Unreal.
Warts and all. Sometimes I played Frankenstein
with the poetry of body parts.

I've had elbows, knees, breasts, toes,
Freudian phallic poems, tossed off
in the guise of other images.
Even belly-buttons have shimmied their way into my heart.

If I've ever been unfaithful to poetry
it's to the rhyming kind – I simply cannot be a couplet
with free verse on my mind!

Letter to an English Aunt

I wonder how the winter is in Kent.
The summerhouse you wrote of last spring
may soon be veiled in snow
and I imagine you'll curl up, instead,
beside the central heating to read.
I picture you in a favourite easy chair,
but what you read, I'll never know.
Your thoughts are a territory I cannot embrace.

Here, in Australia, the days grow slowly warm
but never seem to match the heat of childhood summers gone
when the ripe air smelled of peach and plum,
the gaping cracks of drying creeks.
These impressions do not belong
to the few details you know of my life
yet, you seem to know me well
I sense, beyond knowledge,
a unity awkward to describe.

You've read between my lines
whispered back in silent spaces
a language other than the tongue.

I still have the book of Eliot's poems
you gave as a gift, a decade ago –
its inner covers brushed
with the felt tip flourish of your pen.
Secret messages woven in script,
meaningful quotations copied out,
floral artistry to hide the marks
where its jacket, once taped down, was ripped.
I cherish the feel of its naked blue cloth,
your careful choosing.

You were always the artist. This much I know –
pressing gold leaf to your sacred icons
perhaps, well into the night.
Your egg tempera kitchen of canvasses;
the childish works your mother hoarded,
with the enduring message that stirs me still to tears
'to Mummy, with love'

There's an abstract of yours in the Tate.
I have a drawer full of home-made greetings
but, for all the love of your art,
the letters, cards and icons,
imagination is a deceiving gel
and I can never seem to draw you
from these fragments whole.

Book of Songs

In those early days
there were choices to make
and directions to choose.
Life was in a hurry to unfold
impatience wished the years away
like newspaper pages caught by the wind
taking momentary flight.
All those words and stories
finding sudden wings
hoping to find a comfortable place in the world of dreams.
You had to choose
but choose within the bounds
of school counsellors, parents, society.
You couldn't choose to be a musician
that would have to come later
that was just a dream.
You had to make a living
so you put down your guitar
and burned your book of songs
scribbled from the heart.
You went to business college, learned to type reports
and letters *to whom it may concern*
You were young and the world seemed boundless
but it taught you to conform.
You could walk through many doors
but it was sometimes hard to choose
one that would lead to a version of you.

Many doors would beckon
but so many closed in your face
though so many did make you welcome
you were unsure of your place.
Sometimes the choices are out of your control
they are no choice at all
our instincts get the better of us
but we learn and go on choosing.
In the end, we may learn to do what's best
but for whom? Perhaps we maximise
happiness, create the greatest good
we know we should
be happy and loved
but that depends on the choice of door
and how we shake those ghosts that shadow our paths.
Until one day the sky is clear
we see the clouds for what they are
or what they might become.

We see ourselves, and our choices
and walk back to those early doors
look beyond the dark passages
or look lovingly at memories in the corners of candlelit rooms.
Taste wine and tears and skin,
gently close the eyelids of the dead,
let our dreams rise to the surface
and waft like incense to perfume our remaining days.
Remember we lived and learned and loved and chose,
we hurt and cared and carried on, choosing to live
and when we arrive our regrets may be few
for the choices we made that we cannot undo
that painted our history on the canvas of time.

One way to read poems

Submerged in a bath
in a cloud of scented bubbles
opalescent on skin
hot water raising
the temperature of blood
and emotion
making language
poignant and beautiful
excruciating openness
the naked vulnerability
of tears brushed from lashes
the poems speak
ripples
through amniotic waters
to foetal heart.

I am music

I am music
I am music
I enter the room with percussion
or a gentle rise.
You will feel me beating at skin
or stirring emotion.
I am an ice-blue vein
ticking in your wrist.
I am life
I am music

I remember you
and lead you to places
you've known before.
I am music and memory.
I was there in the room
when you first made love.
I echo your ecstasy
I aid your grief
I will come to your funeral
I am all things to all people
I am music
I am life

I am the loner in the corner
and the dancer in the spotlight.
I am laser beam and strobe
attuned to your mood
I can lift you or sink you
I carry the words
you repeat in my presence
in smoke-wreathed bars
and sun-warmed squares.
I will come to your party
and stay the night
I am life
I am music
an ice-blue vein
ticking in your wrist.
I will make you happy
(or sad)
but will comfort you
and make you dance
in my crescendo.
I am music
I am music, I am music.

Ocean Woman

Your dark hair drowns me.
Our bodies
seaweed tangled.
Wet.
The sea grapes glisten
and my whole heart listens
to the rhythmic wash
of your breath.

Break over the sands of my naked waist.
Your gently foaming hands
your silver fingers.
Make me ripple and swell
in the trembling depths
of your climactic love.

The Conversation of Cooks

Inspired by a line from a Charles Simic poem

The conversation of cooks
feeds the imagination like a good poem.

Well-seasoned,
and packed with the best ingredients,
it mixes well with gossip and laughter

bubbles just on the surface
as a pot of hot soup left to simmer.

Flows from a gravy boat of language.
Great with chopped sentences
and diced metaphors.

Rises like well-aerated soufflés
but always at risk of collapse.

The conversation of cooks
Is rolled out like dough
And cut to shape its audience.

A poem in the making.

Don't read poetry to me

When I hear your voice
reading poetry
I hear, I feel,
the coercive lap of emotion,
its beguiling tow dragging me
into swell, gathering
my body, senses, soul
to raise upon its crest
of tumbled passion
break me down
consume me whole

it is just that ocean
its inevitable rip, I wish to evade
your voice like the brush of soft feathers
on my nape; conscience a gulls cry
not quite swallowed by that shadowy sea.
No, 'Don't!'
Don't read poetry to me.

Shared Music

In the airport lounge
we share your music
through the aural umbilical
of twin ear pieces.

In utero, I played you mine
through a tight drum of skin
felt you shift slightly
with the beat.

Now you're on the move again
flying back to the Gold Coast you call home.
Sixteen years of temporary separations
ought to have toughened me against this…

Later, on the drive home,
I will be grateful for the thread of music
spinning connections from the radio
to bind you close in memory.

Returning

Green stubbled fields wet with dew
inward eyes returning to a place
that floods me with memories
of childhood days, of bliss, and dreaming walks.

The old stone bridge, forgotten all these years,
where, once, I leant toward the moving stream
as it rushed around pebbles, reeds, and stones
in its strange dark alcove of creaking trees;
leaped at butterflies on grassy banks
to the mysterious music of frogs.

Here, I smelt bracken, fennel, and earth.
Now, in my mind, the seasons mix the scents
Of sweet cut hay, manure, pine and rain.

Night Walk

Midnight. We walk
the labyrinth of dark wet streets
and jasmine scent.
Street lamps cast their orange light
into bitumen pools
through a strange theatrics of drizzling rain.

We follow the main street
of our own quiet rhythms
past fluorescent-lit windows
to the dark pulse of the sea.

On the Esplanade,
we lean against pinewood rails,
look out at the ocean.
Its rhythms course through our clasped hands
fusing universe and place
in the chance meeting of our lips
and we return to the untouched
sandhill of our childhood.

Road Poem

To write a poem about a road
you must walk the length of it
until you feel the burn
of hot bitumen under your skin.

You must travel it in sun and rain and wind
feel the sweat of it streaming from armpits
the thirst it inspires
as you move awkwardly along it
like a swimmer who has jumped in fully clothed
longing to peel its tight wetness
from your weighted body
breathing in its outward breath
until the road unwinds in you.

You must dream of what's at the end
like a rainbow you can never reach
or a flimsy stash of hope.

Your thoughts are cars that speed along it
seeking the right exit
sometimes seeing red
so that ideas no longer flow
and you are forced to wait
for a green metaphor.

To write a poem about a road
do you simply lay it down in your mind
letting the bitumen seep into your brain
close your eyes to the open road
and follow the white line of language?

White Mecca 1975

Port Noarlunga

I was thirteen and wore a bikini. I was lean then. We were all lean. We would lean with the steep of the climb. Into the steep. Up the slope. Into sky. I don't remember clouds. Just that glistening sand heap. The ridge of its crest, precise on Mediterranean blue. Everything so precise. We were lean and precise. Our muscles tingled with the climb. No dune grass then. No spinifex to grasp. No grass to grip. Only white and blue before us. Grains of glass glittering in sand. We were cool in dark glasses. Shaz, Carlos and Dazza; the kid they called Fat Albert, and me. All lean, except Albert who would puff up the dune red-faced, dripping sweat, like a pork roast oozing dripping. The only one in jeans. Fat Albert – we all forgot his real name. He never swam. The slide down dunes was his ultimate thrill. We cheered him on. Always the fastest. Shifting his weight for the slide, he excelled. Dragging himself out of the river like a wet blimp. We walked barefoot from Christies to Port Noarlunga. No fear of needles. Along the Esplanade. Up and over the Bluff. Bypassing the jetty. We sought our white Mecca. Our ecstasy. Our ascension. The struggle of climbing. Thrill of the ride. All the way. Over the edge. The cool of the river. Its bed of thick mud swallowed more than our ankles, even then. We joked about bodies of dead cats – growling ghosts – deep down in the suck of mud. Felt their rough tongues on the soles of our feet. Clambered out quickly to the sanctuary of white. We stopped at the kiosk to buy orange frosties. Strip off the sticky paper. Cool our tongues on coloured ice. Remembering how, in winter, the river rose above its banks and flooded the kiosk. The cool concrete floor – a balm for burning feet. There were always sandbags stacked outside. The heat was our god. The sun. Our summer lifestyle.

Hormones. Pulsing in speedos. Our lean teen summer. Whole days climbing that sand dune. As our sun-god travelled across sky. Aching for water. We trekked along dunes, in the rush of voices – the laughing, the squealing. Someone would bring a sheet of masonite, or an old tin signboard, salvaged from a vacant block of land. (We'd brush the snail crust off the tin and use it to slide on.) We climbed the steep white into sky. Again and again. Almost breathless. We were soft shift in glistening sand. We'd queue at the crest of white on blue – a wave of sand – gathering to break over the wetlands, the estuary. Gazing out across the river, the road-bridge, as cars silently ascended and descended the grey bitumen strip of Norwood Hill. Finally, we'd grasp the edge of the sun-hot sheet and bless it like a prayer mat. Shift our weight for the adrenaline slide. Gasp in the air rush, amid the cheering. Down the pristine slope. All the way to the river. Into the splash of dubious water. The shocking cool. The ghosts of dead cats licking our heels.

The End

It will seem odd to sing of the end from where I hope is the middle.
Such things are often left unspoken and who will know if I never tell
that when I die I hope for certain things to go my way
so I may rest in the eternal peace of a soul fitting end, if indeed there be a soul.
I have attended many funerals and heard the mourners say
they hoped the proceedings were as the deceased would have wanted.
I have witnessed the overly Christian tones of an atheist farewell
imagined a grimace from within the polished walls of the coffin.
I have farewelled close family members and been shocked at how little I knew.
I barely knew my mother-in-law (ours was a late marriage) but there was something
beautiful, spiritual, in the moist softness of pink rose petals parting from my fingertips,
the remembrance of Pachelbel's *Canon* in the old, half-empty church
the coffin lowered to reunion with her long dead husband.
Who will be left to think of me, or who will care, when I pass?
My husband? Parents? Children? Beloved grandchildren?
It could happen tomorrow, or in forty years, and maybe I will have changed my mind
but the things I write of here, today, have been set in my thoughts for a decade.

Maybe this is a family trait rising to the surface perhaps too soon, as I know that my father has his funeral mapped out to save us from uncertainty and disorder.
Possibly my need to get this down on paper is prompted by my sister's death at 43
and a nephew's at 21. How unfair seems illness to cut lives so short so swiftly
and suspend them cruelly in comas. The waiting is a sentence on the living, yet kindles hope.

I am not *keen* to go, although I feel I have almost come to terms with death, but I don't wish to linger.
Please, if there is very little hope, turn off the switch and let me sink into sleep, but for your own sake stay within the law. I don't want a mournful sermon to send me off. This is how I hope it will be. Please do your best, those who are left.
First, let the surgeons take my organs, in memory of my sister, if they can improve the lives of others.
I'd like a simple white coffin with no ornamental extravagance. If my hair is still long, let me wear it down. Some flowers would be a nice touch – simple daisies (a small variety) will do. I am a lover of daisy chains.
My husband would say I'm romantic – too romantic – but I know what is important to me and I'd like to lie among nice things before the rot of worms and pessimism sets in. Sorry my love! It is true what Eliot said – *humankind cannot bear too much reality*
though I have my realistic streak too. I have learned that too much realism is unkind to the spirit.

Dress me in a long flowing dress of soft, simple cotton in
white or blue or saffron, perhaps a little embroidery.
And no shoes or underwear! I insist on bare feet and no
knicker line! And let my breasts fall free!
I'd like to wear my wedding ring and earrings that dangle and
sparkle, but no necklaces please!
I think it would be symbolic to send me into the flames
with a book clasped to my chest, and there is only one that
carries a weight of meaning – the blue bound volume of T.S.
Eliot (1962) given to me by my auntie. You'll find it on a
bookshelf somewhere. I'll become ash with 'Burnt Norton'.
Let me be; it's amusing!

As for make-up, although there will be no one to see it I
think it will hide the pallor of grey.
But keep it simple and understated – no bright lipstick! Just a
subtle shade of muted berry to keep my lips moist.
If you discover my strange habit of keeping my children's
lost teeth, and find them scattered throughout my drawers
in little boxes and envelopes…or the sachet of hair from my
son's first cut…I think I can finally part with these.
I won't take them with me! I'll be in the mood for letting go
of life's little oddities and mother comforts.
My service should take place outside if I am lucky enough to
go in spring, or the cooler part of summer.
I prefer a cathedral of trees and the openness of sky to the
trappings and plastic fernery of a chapel.
Keep it short and simple. Let only a few determined speakers
tell of their memories. That is all very well and perhaps
necessary if there is grieving, but I'm keen to have some
poetry, so please… Poets come and read.

Send me off (not up) with verses and bring a guitar…even better a saxophone.
There's only one bit of the Bible I'll be happy to have read – 1 Corinthians 13:1–13 – and when it gets to the part
'When I became a man…' please do me a favour and say 'woman'. I am what I am.
I've already made it clear that music and poetry should be invited to the service but please bring me a Buddhist monk with bells and gongs and chants. And a prayer on the Four Immeasurables – Love, Compassion, Joy and Equanimity. Scented flowers are beautiful to me – like roses, jasmine and tropical frangipani – so cover my coffin with these and imagine me smiling as I lie in wait for the furnace. I will be happy. Don't feel that afterwards the guests should take tea as I was not a drinker. Drink wine or beer and be merry!

When the ashes have been raked and bottled I hope that someone will drive me to my resting place of choice and scatter me in three.
Part of me will go to my husband. If he should go before me scatter a third at his resting place and water me in.
If still living he may wish to hold me for a while. Two thirds of me should be driven to Moorook and scattered at a part of the Murray where there's a rose garden beside the river. Pour me over the roses and I will enter their roots.
The final portion should go into the river where pelicans nest and I shall return to the epiphany of my youth
whatever it was that remained with me all those years. From the time I was 16 and a group of us slept in cars beside the water.

When I woke, the morning was supernatural with mist. It was bitter cold. My clothes were damp. I stood in the early light and watched a pelican rise into the white wisps of daybreak. I don't know what happened but I was unexpectedly one, with trees, birds, river, mist
and as I write this it still stirs my solar plexus, catches in my throat and induces a tear.
I don't know what it was but that's how I'd like to end.
Returning to a sacred morning. Ash to earth. Ash to water. In my element.

www.ingramcontent.com/pod-product-compliance
Lightning Source LLC
Chambersburg PA
CBHW070907080526
44589CB00013B/1203